55070
Leach Library

LEACH LIBRARY
276 Mammoth Road
Londonderry, NH 03053
432-1127

DISCARD

Leach Library
276 Mammoth Road
Londonderry, NH   03053

Adult Services 432-1132
Children's Services 432-1127

GAYLORD

Norman Rockwell

Norman Rockwell
AMERICA'S BEST-LOVED ILLUSTRATOR

BY JOEL H. COHEN

A First Book

FRANKLIN WATTS · A DIVISION OF GROLIER PUBLISHING
NEW YORK · LONDON · HONG KONG · SYDNEY · DANBURY, CONNECTICUT

J
BIO
ROC

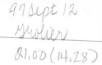

97 Sept 12
Grolier
21.00 (14.28)

For Nancy

ACKNOWLEDGMENTS

SPECIAL THANKS TO TOM ROCKWELL AND PETER ROCKWELL; LINDA SZEKELY, ASSISTANT CURATOR, AND OTHER STAFF MEMBERS AND VOLUNTEERS AT THE NORMAN ROCKWELL MUSEUM AT STOCKBRIDGE; THE *BERKSHIRE EAGLE* (GRACE MCMAHON, LIBRARIAN); THE ROCKWELL MODELS WHO SHARED THEIR EXPERIENCES, AND, FOR HER THOUGHTFUL, INVALUABLE EDITING HELP, ANN COHEN.

Cover and interior design: Michelle Regan

Photographs ©: Brown & Bigelow, Inc.: 16; The Curtis Publishing Company: 19, 34; Courtesy of The Norman Rockwell Museum at Stockbridge: 37, 53 (Louie Lamone), 39, 43 (Gene Pelham), cover, back cover, 2, 7, 8, 10, 12, 13, 14, 18, 21, 23, 25, 26, 28, 30, 32, 38, 41, 45, 46, 47, 48, 50, 52, 55, 58, UPI/Corbis-Bettmann: 29, 36.

Library of Congress Cataloging-in-Publication Data
Cohen, Joel H.
    Norman Rockwell : America's best-loved illustrator / Joel H. Cohen.
        p. cm. — (A First book)
    Includes bibliographical references and index.
    Summary: A biography of the painter who for sixty-five years portrayed America for Americans as they liked to see themselves.
       ISBN 0-531-20266-6 (lib.bdg.)   0-516-15840-3 (pbk.)
    1. Rockwell, Norman, 1894–1978—Juvenile literature. 2. Painters—United States—Biography—Juvenile literature. [1. Rockwell, Norman, 1894–1978. 2. Artists.] I. Title. II. Series.
ND237.R68C65 1997
759.13—dc20
[B]   96-35103
                                                        CIP
                                                         AC

© 1997 by Joel H. Cohen
All rights reserved. Printed simultaneously in Canada
Printed in the United States of America
1 2 3 4 5 6 7 8 9 10 R 06 05 04 03 02 01 00 99 98 97

CONTENTS

CHAPTER ONE

"The Best Idea I Ever Had"

One summer night in 1942, Norman Rockwell leaped out of bed with what he would later call "the best idea I ever had."

The nation was in the thick of World War II, and Norman had been mulling over how to paint President Franklin D. Roosevelt's lofty ideals for postwar peace, which Roosevelt called "the four freedoms." Norman wanted to illustrate these freedoms in a way that was understandable and meaningful to all Americans.

It had come to him suddenly, after remembering a town meeting at which a neighbor had been allowed to have his say even though everyone disagreed with him. Norman Rockwell decided to use his neighbors as models to illustrate the four freedoms. His paintings would show four

FREEDOM OF SPEECH

FREEDOM OF RELIGION

FREEDOM FROM WANT

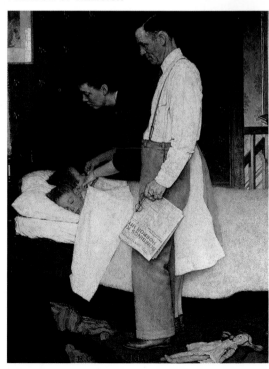

FREEDOM FROM FEAR

scenes: a New England town meeting in *Freedom of Speech*, a Thanksgiving dinner in *Freedom from Want*, people of different faiths praying in *Freedom of Religion*, and a couple tucking their children into bed in *Freedom from Fear*.

But when Norman Rockwell took the illustrations to Washington, D.C., one government agency after another turned them down. Dejected, he headed home, stopping in Philadelphia to discuss cover ideas with the editor of the *Saturday Evening Post*. Norman Rockwell was a favorite at the *Post*, the country's most popular weekly family magazine at the time. When the editor saw Norman's sketches, he told Norman to drop everything else and finish them.

After the pictures were published in the *Post* in 1943, the U.S. Treasury Department sent them on a nationwide tour, which helped raise more than 132 million dollars in war-bond sales. The Office of War Information, which had told Norman that it wanted "*real* artists," not illustrators, to complete the posters, issued more than four million prints of his series. The public received the paintings, in one writer's words, "with more enthusiasm, perhaps, than any other paintings in the history of American art."

The *Four Freedoms* differed from Norman Rockwell's usual cheerful, often humorous view of middle-class American life: a grinning tomboy with a black eye outside a prin-

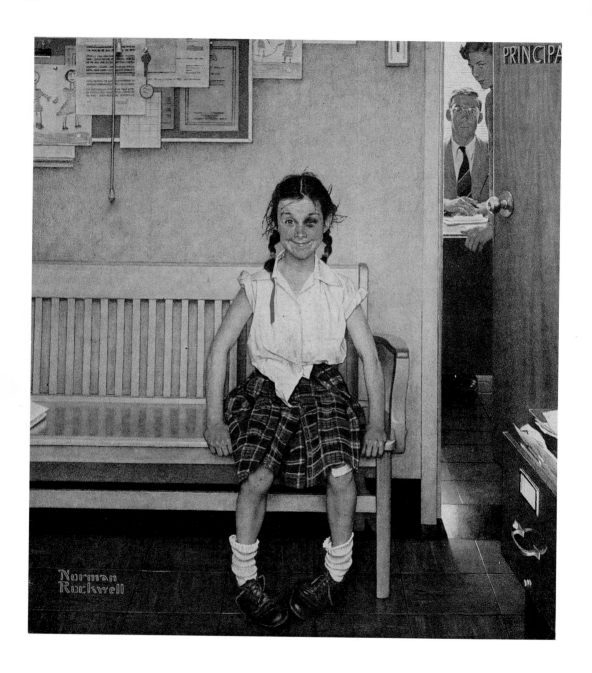

cipal's office; a bare-bottomed boy who, about to get a shot, is examining the doctor's diploma; a middle-aged man skinny-dipping; a doctor examining a girl's "sick" doll with a stethoscope.

But whatever the subject, Norman Rockwell celebrated kindness, decency, friendship, family ties, and patriotism in his illustrations. He painted America at its best.

NORMAN ROCKWELL'S HUMOROUS STYLE CAN BE SEEN
IN ILLUSTRATIONS SUCH AS *GIRL WITH BLACK EYE*,
PUBLISHED ON THE COVER OF THE *SATURDAY EVENING
POST* IN 1953.

CHAPTER TWO

City Boy, Country Dreams

"The story of my life is, really, the story of my pictures and how I made them. Because, in one way or another, everything I have ever seen or done has gone into my pictures," Norman Rockwell once explained.

You might guess from his illustrations that Norman grew up a country boy. In fact, it was in a New York City brownstone that Norman Percevel Rockwell was born on February 3, 1894, the second of two sons of Nancy and Jarvis Waring Rockwell. According to Norman, "we were just a nice family."

On winter evenings, at the dining-room table, illuminated by gaslight, Norman's father would read the novels of Charles Dickens to Norman and his brother, Jarvis. Norman would draw pictures of Mr. Micawber, Oliver Twist, and

12

YOUNG NORMAN (SECOND FROM TOP) WITH HIS PARENTS AND BROTHER JARVIS IN ABOUT 1904

other Dickens characters. "Dickens had an awful lot to do with me, because he wrote about the kind of people I painted," Norman said.

"I think I've always wanted to be an artist. I certainly can't remember ever wanting to be anything else," Norman explained.

A choirboy who participated in his share of pranks, Norman Rockwell had an enjoyable childhood. As a youth, however, Norman was troubled about things, particularly his gawky appearance and bulging Adam's apple. His mother called him "Snow-in-the-Face" because he was so pale, and some kids called him "Mooney" because he wore round, rimless eyeglasses. Norman was also embarrassed by his pigeon toes and spaghetti arms. Sometimes he would try to make people feel sorry for him by limping or pulling his sleeve down so people would think he had just one hand. It didn't seem fair to Norman that he completely lacked athletic ability while his brother excelled at sports.

"All I had was the ability to draw, which as far as I could see didn't count for much," he recalled. "But because it was all I had, I began to make it my whole life. I drew all the time. . . . [And] gradually my narrow shoulders, long neck, and pigeon toes became less important to me."

Influences on his art were everywhere. The Rockwells passed their summers on farms in upstate New York. Norman's fond memories of the country contrasted with his memories of the city's filth and crime. "The clean air, the green fields, the thousand and one things to do . . . changed our personalities as much as the sun changed the color of our skins. . . . The summers I spent in the country as a child . . . had a lot to do with

NORMAN (RIGHT) AND A FRIEND PLAY WITH FROGS DURING A SUMMER VACATION IN UPSTATE NEW YORK.

what I painted later on." Later, when his mother became too ill for housework, Norman's family lived in boardinghouses, whose sad, quirky owners and residents made a lasting impression on Norman.

Although Norman did not feel very close to his parents, they supported his art ambitions. When Norman was a freshman in high school, they arranged for him to take art lessons every Saturday at the Chase School of Art in New York City. By this time, the Rockwells had moved to Mamaroneck, New York, and Norman had to travel two hours by trolley and subway to reach the school.

An undistinguished student at Mamaroneck High, Norman dropped out in his second year to enter the National Academy School. Not long after, he switched to the Art Students League, where he thrived. Norman, however, seemed so solemn that schoolmates nicknamed him "The Deacon." Even then Norman was very serious about his art. With two other students, he signed an oath in blood that they would always try for the highest standards in art and never earn more than fifty dollars a week.

Norman earned tuition for school in many ways. He delivered mail on his bicycle for twenty-five cents a day, appeared as an extra at the Metropolitan Opera with the great tenor Enrico Caruso, and gave actress Ethel Barrymore art lessons. A teacher helped Norman get drawing assign-

As art director at the Boy Scout magazine *Boys' Life*, Norman completed hundreds of illustrations, including *A Scout Is Helpful*.

16

ments: tombstone inscriptions for a catalog, which he jokingly based on living classmates, and book illustrations for *Tell-Me-Why Stories*.

This project led to illustrating a hiking handbook for the editor of the Boy Scout magazine *Boys' Life* in 1912. The editor was so pleased with the work, he later made Norman, who was hardly older than its readers, the magazine's art director. Norman illustrated Boy Scout handbooks and painted almost every Boy Scout calendar from the mid-1920s to 1978.

One Boy Scout whom Norman inspired is now the movie director Steven Spielberg. Spielberg discovered Norman Rockwell's artistry in a poster he saw at weekly Boy Scout meetings in Scottsdale, Arizona. Titled *The Spirit of America*, it featured an "older, nobler" Scout, with Presidents Lincoln and Washington in the background. It "gave us an image to aspire toward," said Spielberg, who owns *Spirit* and several other Norman Rockwell originals.

Norman also received large fees for completing print advertisements for socks, life insurance, corn flakes, soft drinks, toothpaste, and cough medicine. But what mattered most to Norman Rockwell was his art. In his studio in New Rochelle, New York, he painted a rating scale from "excellent" to "bad" and "100%" in gold on the top of his easel as a reminder to do his very best.

CHAPTER THREE

Norman "Arrives"

For an illustrator, the "greatest show window in America," Norman Rockwell once said, was the cover of the *Saturday Evening Post*. "If you did a cover for the *Post* you had arrived."

A cartoonist friend encouraged the young Norman to try for a *Post* cover. When *Post* editor George Horace Lorimer bought two finished pieces and approved three sketches for future covers for seventy-five dollars each, Norman could barely contain his excitement. He immediately proposed marriage to Irene O'Connor, and she accepted. (They divorced fourteen years later.)

Norman Rockwell was just twenty-two years old when his first *Post* cover, *Boy with Baby Carriage*, appeared on

BOY WITH BABY CARRIAGE WAS THE FIRST OF NORMAN ROCKWELL'S MORE THAN 320 *SATURDAY EVENING POST* COVERS.

May 20, 1916. In the painting, a dressed-up boy with a baby bottle in his pocket and pushing a baby carriage is taunted by friends on their way to play ball. Over the next forty-seven years, Norman Rockwell would do more than 320 *Saturday Evening Post* covers and 158 story illustrations. His work became so popular that whenever the *Post* had a Norman Rockwell painting on its cover, it printed a quarter of a million extra copies.

A wonderful storyteller who used images and details to great effect, Norman Rockwell painted everyday situations that people could identify with. To the delight of millions, he painted average Americans in a way that evoked sympathy, admiration, and usually a smile or chuckle. As one writer put it: "He made the average American special."

Some of his works were just funny: an overweight chef eats pastry while reading a diet book; a sailor has the name of his current girlfriend tattooed on his arm, under the crossed-out names of past loves; and partially clothed boys run from a swimming hole past a "no swimming" sign. Norman Rockwell, however, believed that while pure gags were good, funny ideas combined with other emotions were better.

"People somehow get out of your work just about what you put into it," he said, "and if you are interested in the characters that you draw, and understand them and love

THE DISCOVERY, A NORMAN ROCKWELL ILLUSTRATION FOR A 1956 *POST* COVER

them, the person who sees your picture is bound to feel the same way." Whether it was a painting of a youngster shocked to discover Santa's costume in his father's dresser in *The Discovery* or of men playing music in a back room in *Shuffleton's Barbershop*, Norman Rockwell's works had universal appeal.

Real life wasn't always quite as idyllic as Norman Rockwell painted it. "I sometimes think we paint to fulfill ourselves and our lives, to supply the things we want and don't have. . . . I paint life as I would like it to be," he said.

Two years after his first *Post* cover, in 1918, with the United States at war, Norman decided to enlist in the Navy. At the recruiting office, however, the skinny artist was told he was below the minimum weight for acceptance. In order to enlist, he needed to gain seven pounds. So, following the navy doctor's prescription, he stuffed himself with bananas, doughnuts, and water for hours until he had gained the required weight.

Norman Rockwell, "painter and varnisher, third class," was sent to South Carolina. He helped the war effort by doing portraits of navy officers, their wives, and noncommissioned sailors.

Norman was soon eager to return to civilian life. Because no honorable discharges were issued at the time, he was "discharged with inaptitude" with the OK of his commanding officer. His service record noted that Norman was "an artist and unaccustomed to hard manual labor."

But Norman, an artist who sometimes wore out canvases with do-overs, was no stranger to hard work. He was a compulsive worker who painted every day, even Christmas. In a career of some sixty-five years, he completed over four thou-

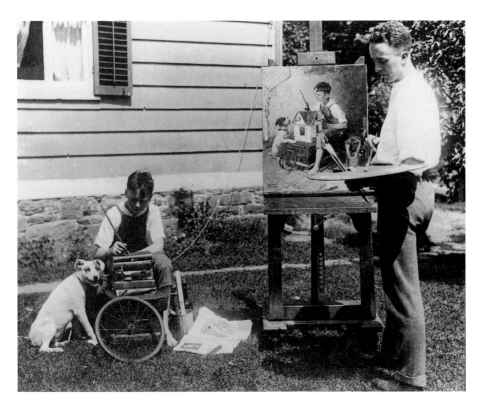

AFTER HIS STINT IN THE NAVY, NORMAN RETURNED TO HIS TRUE CALLING—PAINTING. AT HIS EASEL, HE WORKS FROM A COUPLE OF LIVE MODELS.

sand works of art, including nearly four hundred covers, calendars, and portraits of U.S. presidents and such celebrities as John Wayne and Colonel Sanders. From the cheerfulness, volume, and popularity of his work, you might think Norman Rockwell was a carefree, self-confident illustrator who just dashed off his chuckle-inspiring paintings.

Norman Rockwell, however, was a complex man, deadly serious about his art. He was a stickler for authenticity and a meticulous craftsman whose paintings show careful observation and technical skill. In fact, in later years, despite his esteemed reputation, Norman Rockwell enrolled in a weekly sketching class to loosen his style and help him create more natural paintings.

A student of the classical painters, Norman Rockwell often incorporated their techniques—the lighting, proportion, and minute detail—in his work. Well-read and knowledgeable about art history, he took numerous trips to Europe to study the old masters firsthand (Rembrandt was a particular favorite).

Even Norman Rockwell's most lighthearted works were carefully thought out and executed. David H. Wood, former director of the Norman Rockwell Museum in Stockbridge, Massachusetts, said of the artist: "He was always . . . nagged by the sense that 'there must be something more than I'm

THE SATURDAY EVENING

POST

APRIL 29, 1950   15¢

I ESCAPED OVER THE
ROOF OF THE WORLD
A U.S. Consul's Own Story
of His Flight From the Reds

SHUFFLETON'S BARBERSHOP, A 1950 *POST* COVER DISPLAYS NORMAN ROCKWELL'S
MASTERFUL USE OF LIGHT IN HIS PAINTINGS.

NORMAN ROCKWELL SAID HE COULDN'T HELP CARICATURING THE FACES IN THIS 1957 *POST* COVER, *AFTER THE PROM*.

putting down on this canvas.' He had probably less self-esteem than anyone I've ever known."

Norman Rockwell wanted everyone to like his work. He used to ask people who came to his studio, regardless of their knowledge of art, to comment on his paintings. "If they don't understand what I'm trying to say, a lot of other people won't either," he explained. Norman would often still do the painting as he saw fit.

Even when his work was well received he had second thoughts: "I often caricature when I shouldn't. I fail to see the people as real people. I oversimplify. I try to make them too cute."

Magazine readers and editors didn't seem to agree, and Norman Rockwell eventually painted for twenty national publications. He remained loyal to the *Post*, even though a new magazine offered to double his price. When *Post* editor Lorimer asked what he intended to do, Norman said, "Stay with the *Post*." "In that case," replied Lorimer, "*we'll* double your price."

CHAPTER FOUR

Family and Work

In 1930, Norman was thirty-six years old and living as a confirmed bachelor. That year, however, he was introduced to a charming, twenty-two-year-old schoolteacher named Mary Rhodes Barstow in California. Two weeks later, Norman proposed. The couple were married on April 17, 1930.

A loving wife, Mary helped Norman over his periods of self-doubt and took an active role in his career. She served as his secretary, read classics and best-sellers to him while he painted, and procured props for his posing sessions. She also kept busy raising their three sons: Jarvis, now an artist, born in 1932; Tom, a writer (and author of the popular children's book *How to Eat Fried Worms*), born in 1933; and Peter, a sculptor, born in 1936.

After a long stay in Europe, the Rockwells moved to a

farm in Arlington, Vermont, a town with a population of twelve hundred. It was just the kind of peaceful, neighborly place Norman had dreamed about as a child.

In 1943, just two nights after Norman sent off the last of the *Four Freedoms* to the *Saturday Evening Post*, there was an urgent pounding at his door and a shout: "The studio's on fire!" By the time firemen arrived, the blaze had destroyed the studio and collections of pipes, props, costumes, brushes, paintings, and sketches—as well as prints by Howard Pyle, an illustrator Norman idolized. "Well, there goes my life's work," said Norman, who illustrated the event for the *Post*.

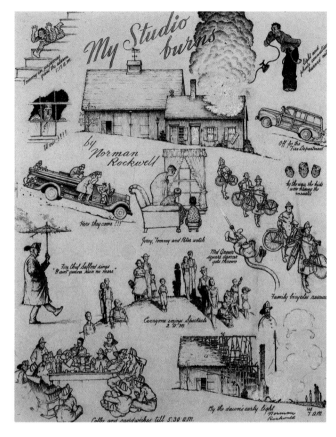

NORMAN MADE LIGHT OF THE DESTRUCTION OF HIS WORKROOM AND ITS CONTENTS IN THIS ILLUSTRATION.

The Rockwells bought a house in nearby West Arlington, where Norman had the destroyed studio rebuilt with help from friends and the Society of Illustrators. With a huge globe and magazine collection, the studio was a fun place for the boys to visit and watch their father paint. Except when he was concentrating extra hard—and then he might be a little sharp with a son dropping in to show a frog—Norman liked having people in his studio. Norman even kept his cool when one of the boys knocked a baseball through the studio window.

For recreation, Norman took walks and played badminton or tennis, in long pants to hide his skinny legs. Occasionally, he dug up dandelions. Evenings, he would methodically rip and pile up diapers to be used as paint rags.

A good teller of jokes and stories, Norman liked amusing his sons with anecdotes from his childhood, poems such as Leigh Hunt's "Abou Ben Adhem," and limericks. The Rockwell dinner table became the scene of teasing and friendly arguments, along with reports of Norman's work, art, and the day's news. Because Norman worked constantly, family outings and vacations were rare. Still, he provided excitement with spontaneous trips to the circus or California by train.

Was Norman Rockwell a painter or illustrator? "I call myself an illustrator because my pictures tell a story," he said. "Of course, if someone calls me an artist, I don't argue."

He preferred doing covers because "I like to tell my own stories." Yet he was delighted to be asked to illustrate special editions of Mark Twain's *Tom Sawyer* and *Huckleberry Finn* in 1935. Norman visited Twain's hometown of Hanni-

NORMAN AND MARY ROCKWELL'S SONS (FROM LEFT TO RIGHT): THOMAS, JARVIS, AND PETER IN ARLINGTON, VERMONT

bal, Missouri, to see the cave, schoolroom, and other sites described in the novels.

Seeking authentic, well-worn, and naturally aged clothing for the project, Norman gave a farmer his hat, trousers, and jacket in exchange for the farmer's patched overalls—and bought him a new outfit as well. The next day, a crowd approached with bundles of moth-eaten clothing because there had been a report of a "crazy man" buying old clothes for high prices!

Most of Norman's work continued to be for the *Post*, which had undergone changes. Norman brought nine sketches to the magazine's new editor, Ben Hibbs. When Hibbs wanted all of them, Norman almost fainted with surprise.

Norman Rockwell compared starting a painting to "jumping into an ice-cold bath" and always felt his best—a "wow"—was the one he would paint next. Whenever he was asked which was his favorite work, like Pablo Picasso he would cite the one he was working on.

World War II was fertile ground for Norman Rockwell's special touch. He portrayed the conflict in understandable human terms and often humorously. He focused on the individual serviceman or more often, the people back home—men in a lunchroom listening to a radio account of the D-Day invasion, women war workers, and a returned soldier peeling potatoes (a hated army chore) for his mother. And, as the war drew to an end, Norman painted homecomings.

One of his most popular series of World War II covers dealt with the experiences of Willie Gillis, an imaginary soldier, from his induction through his service overseas, enjoying doughnuts at a USO, doing kitchen duty, and sleeping late on furlough under a "Home Sweet Home" sign. The series continued even after the model, Bob Buck, a Vermont sawmill worker whom Norman discovered at a square dance, joined the Navy!

One of the few suggestions for a painting Norman took from anyone resulted in *Saying Grace*, which millions of *Post* readers voted their favorite Norman Rockwell cover. It depicted an old woman and young boy praying in a diner while puzzled—but respectful, as Norman saw it—people looked on.

In 1952, the *Post*, which had been asking Norman to

SATURDAY EVENING POST READERS VOTED *SAYING GRACE* THEIR FAVORITE NORMAN ROCKWELL COVER.

paint people in the news instead of "average Americans," had an urgent assignment: a portrait of President Dwight D. Eisenhower. Norman had less than twenty-four hours to reach the vacationing president in Denver, Colorado. Desperately tired and nervous, Norman was escorted to the president's suite. He found Eisenhower considerate and patient —as "comfortable as an old shoe," with "the most expressive face I've ever painted."

In 1953, Norman felt an urge to move, believing a change of scenery would help his work. Also, stress had begun to affect Mary's health. To be closer to a center that could provide psychiatric help, the Rockwells moved to Stockbridge, Massachusetts, where Norman occasionally had counseling, too.

Wherever he lived, the artist, tall and skinny (despite a big appetite for things like peanut butter, ice cream, and pie), became a familiar, beloved figure. Everyone liked him, partly because he was so intent on having everyone like him.

"I prefer living near the community, not isolated from it," Norman said. "Makes it easier to visit and to be visited." One tourist took him literally and climbed in Norman's bedroom window. Other interruptions resulted in a sign: "Working Studio. No Visitors Please."

Norman's first studio in Stockbridge was above a

NORMAN AT WORK IN HIS STUDIO

meat market in the town center. A big second-floor window let in northern light and allowed him to spot potential models below. When the Rockwells moved from Main Street to a nearby white clapboard house, Norman had a nineteenth-century red carriage barn remodeled into what he considered his best studio, which he kept characteristically neat.

Life seemed trouble-free, until one summer day in 1959 when Norman tried to wake Mary from a nap and discovered that she had died. Norman and Mary had been happily married twenty-eight years, and her loss left him deeply depressed.

Unhappy and lonely, he joined a weekly poetry reading club organized by Molly Punderson, a retired English teacher. On October 25, 1961, Molly and Norman were mar-

IN THEIR LATER YEARS, NORMAN AND HIS THIRD WIFE, MOLLY, RODE BICYCLES DAILY IN STOCKBRIDGE, MASSACHUSETTS.

ried. "I don't know how I would have made it if it hadn't been for Molly," he observed.

The couple became known for midday bike rides, a pastime Norman enjoyed into his late seventies. They would bike to Main Street to see friends and up what they called Cardiac Hill.

Norman called his continuing compulsion to work "just a bad habit," noting "I work from exhaustion to exhaustion. There's only so much daylight left."

CHAPTER FIVE

The Joys of Modeling

"If Rockwell hadn't been a master storyteller-in-print," wrote Kenneth Stuart, "he could have been a marvelous actor." Stuart, who became the *Post's* art editor in 1944, was referring to Norman's ability to act out for his models the exact expression he wanted—scrunching up his face at the prospect of bad-tasting cough syrup, for instance.

In a posing session, Norman would patiently explain the story of the painting. He would request different poses and ask the model to make a face "like sucking lemons" or to "raise your eyebrows way up," sometimes pulling up the model's eyebrows himself!

Although he approached his work seriously, posing sessions were always fun for the models. Norman would joke and mug to relax them. Most looked forward to posing for

In this 1949 photograph, Norman Rockwell shows a young model the expression he wants.

him. In one town, it was a legitimate excuse to get out of school.

"There was always music in the studio," recalled one model, Anne Lamone White, whose father, Louis Lamone, was Norman Rockwell's photographer and all-around helper. "It was more fun posing for him than going to the movies," another model recalled. "He loved working with people and that reflects in his work," said Claire Williams, who appeared in three Norman Rockwell ads.

Norman was always in need of models and scouted for them during local square dances, on the street, behind counters, even on tractors. He once left his own anniversary party to enlist a prospect. "I use all my neighbors as models; there is almost nobody in town I haven't painted," Norman Rockwell once said. Most of his models cooperated perfectly. And in one case where the model was too young to cooperate himself, his mother did. She stuck her happy baby with a pin to make him cry, as was required for the painting.

Getting animal models to cooperate was more difficult. Norman would sometimes give a cat a whiff of ether to make it drowsy, shake a chicken from side to side to quiet it, or bang a stick on the wall to make animals turn their heads. He once had a butcher tack a duck's feet (through a painless part of the webbing) to the floor. Other times, he chased a

In *Triple Self-Portrait*, Norman Rockwell pokes fun at vanity and growing old, painting a younger version of himself with better eyesight.

temperamental donkey down a busy avenue and pursued a turkey through town with a young model in Puritan costume.

Frequently, Norman himself modeled. In his *Triple Self-Portrait*, he smokes his ever present pipe, looking at himself in a mirror while painting himself without glasses and younger than his reflection. Attached to the canvas are reproductions of self-portraits by Rembrandt, Van Gogh, and Picasso.

Members of his family also modeled, primarily his three sons. Jarvis and Peter were in the prize-winning *Homecoming Marine*. Tom modeled as the child in *Little Boy Reaching in Grandfather's Overcoat*, among other covers. Being a Rockwell child had its price. While other children got two dollars or more for posing, Norman's young sons were paid just a dollar.

Norman always insisted on paying his models. Longtime friend Jane Fitzpatrick still has the check she got for posing. Children, however, were more interested in cash than checks. And since kids tend to be fidgety, Norman came up with an idea to keep his child models interested. At the beginning of a session he would stack up nickels (or, for younger children, pennies). At each rest period, he would move five coins to the other side of the table as payment.

Norman painted directly from his models for about

NORMAN ROCKWELL PAINTED FROM THIS PHOTOGRAPH OF ONE OF HIS FAVORITE MODELS IN 1954. HE SAID OF *GIRL AT THE MIRROR*: "I SHOULD NOT HAVE ADDED THE PHOTOGRAPH OF THE MOVIE STAR. THE LITTLE GIRL IS NOT WONDERING IF SHE LOOKS LIKE THE STAR, BUT JUST TRYING TO ESTIMATE HER OWN CHARMS."

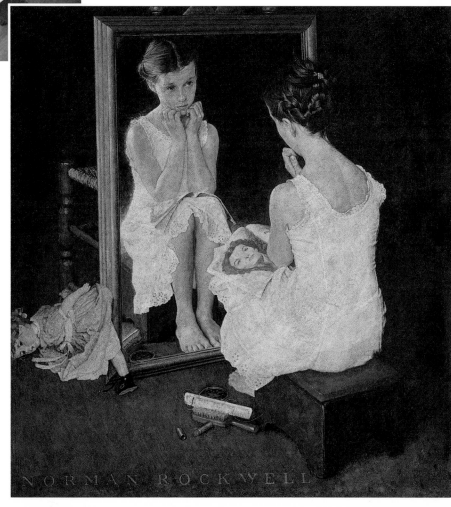

twenty-five years. But the strain of working eight hours with live models, constantly urging them to "smile bigger" or "raise the arm more," left him exhausted. Norman started having the models photographed instead. They didn't have to pose as long, and the camera could catch fresh expressions and details. He directed modeling sessions while a professional took dozens of photos.

Norman Rockwell, who "made it a rule never to fake anything," continued to insist on authenticity. Whenever he had a question of historical accuracy—say, about a nineteenth-century hat—he would consult Polly Pierce, a local historian. And he would visit the scene for "some detail I've forgotten that will make the illustration ring true."

When he planned the *Post* cover of the tomboy with the shiner, Norman offered five dollars to any boy or girl with "a ripe black eye." He did, however, reject a father's offer to give his daughter one if he would choose her as the model.

CHAPTER SIX

New Challenges

In the 1960s, Norman Rockwell faced up to an unpleasant truth: "The kind of thing I did for years is through. The public doesn't want my type of gentle humor anymore, and the magazines don't want it."

Magazines asked him to do types of painting other than his trademark human-interest stories. The *Post* sent him around the world to paint political leaders, something he didn't particularly enjoy. His assigned portrait of Yugoslavia's Marshal Tito wasn't used. Feeling that the *Post* didn't value his work anymore, Norman severed ties after completing his portrait of Jacqueline Kennedy in October 1963. (Years later, when the *Post* was reintroduced as a quarterly, Norman accepted an invitation to pose for a photograph with a boy selling the *Post* for the cover.)

NORMAN ROCKWELL PUTS THE FINISHING TOUCHES ON *THE PROBLEM WE ALL LIVE WITH* IN 1963.

Meanwhile, other major magazines, such as *Look* and *McCall's*, sought Norman out to illustrate subjects that concerned the nation. "There was a change in the thought climate in America brought on by scientific advance, the atom bomb, two world wars, and Mr. Freud and psychology. . . . Now I am wildly excited about painting contemporary sub-

In the 1960s, Norman Rockwell turned to international topics, such as *Peace Corps (JFK's Bold Legacy)*, in which John F. Kennedy appears.

jects . . . pictures about civil rights, astronauts, Peace Corps, the poverty program. It is wonderful."

Several of Norman Rockwell's efforts were among the civil rights movement's more powerful artistic statements. In 1964, for example, Norman did an illustration for *Look* on the effects of school integration. He decided to base it on an

THE PROBLEM WE ALL LIVE WITH, A 1964 PAINTING FOR *LOOK* MAGAZINE

actual instance of state officials defying the Supreme Court by refusing to let African-American students into an all-white school. *The Problem We All Live With* depicts a young black girl in a starched dress being escorted into an all-white school by four federal marshals. She walks past a tomato-splattered wall on which a racial insult has been written.

For the illustration, Norman selected nine-year-old Lynda Gunn as the model. During the posing session, he patiently positioned Lynda's feet on wooden blocks to give the appearance of walking. Today, Gunn remembers Norman Rockwell as "very comfortable to be with, like family." She also recalls bicycling to the museum to look at the painting and thinking, "Boy, that's me." Proud to have been selected, Gunn is "glad it came across with the impact that it did."

Lynda's cousin, Elaine S. Gunn, whose two daughters were recruited as models by Norman, remembers the artist knocking at her door and politely—and unnecessarily—introducing himself. The artist asked whether her daughter, Anita, might pose for him and chatted about what he intended to paint.

About three years later, Norman Rockwell used a second daughter, Tracey, and a cousin, Ray, as the models for *New Kids in the Neighborhood*. The image shows a young

SOUTHERN JUSTICE, A SKETCH COMPLETED IN 1964, WAS A DEPARTURE IN STYLE AND SUBJECT MATTER FOR NORMAN ROCKWELL.

African-American brother and sister exchanging glances with white children in the white neighborhood where their family is moving.

As the struggle for racial equality grew uglier, a solemn Norman Rockwell painting, *Southern Justice*, completed for *Look* in 1964, commemorated the murder of three civil-rights workers in Mississippi. Such was the impact of Norman Rockwell's impressionistic sketch, in brown with red bloodstains, that it was selected instead of his finished painting.

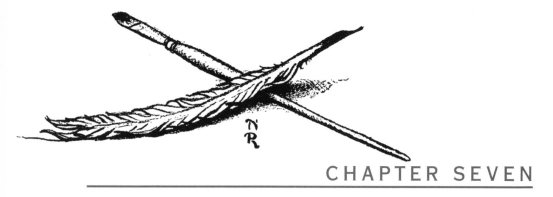

CHAPTER SEVEN

Honoring the Artist

Throughout his career, Norman Rockwell received bushels of fan mail, which he usually responded to with a form letter because of the volume. Honors poured in as well. When a major honor, the Presidential Medal of Freedom, was awarded by President Gerald Ford in January 1977, Norman was in failing health.

Age had begun to catch up with him, and two bike falls were a sign of things to come. He was beginning to nap more frequently, and his memory was failing to the point where he would sometimes not recognize friends or forget an assignment or its subject. He was barely producing any art and what he was producing wasn't up to his usual standards.

Norman Rockwell was eighty-two when *American Artist*,

NORMAN ROCKWELL HOLDING THE
PRESIDENTIAL MEDAL OF FREEDOM,
WHICH HE WAS AWARDED IN 1977

for which he had done one of its first covers in 1940, asked him to do a cover celebrating the nation's bicentennial in 1976. The painting, a self-portrait of the artist tying a ribbon on the Liberty Bell, turned out to be his last.

Norman Rockwell, who had once said "When I die, I want to be working on a picture and just fall over," passed away on November 8, 1978. His death came half a year after, wheelchair-bound, he had last painted. The unfinished final work—depicting a conversation between a Stockbridge colonial missionary and a Native American chief in the mission house—remained on his easel.

Norman Rockwell was buried in Stockbridge Cemetery,

after a funeral at St. Paul's Episcopal Church on his beloved Main Street.

* * *

Norman Rockwell's memory lives on in many ways. His art has been displayed in department store windows, celebrated in a host of collectibles, and even commemorated on U.S. postage stamps. Despite criticisms of his work as too sugar-coated or corny, many consider him America's best-known and best-loved artist.

One writer said Norman Rockwell captured "what was real for Americans, or at least what Americans wanted and hoped and prayed *could* be real." In the process, wrote another, he "delighted, amused and touched more people than any other painter."

"The Norman Rockwell portrayal of our people always hit the bull's-eye, whether it was a Boy Scout, a ballplayer, or some other typical character on the American scene," President Ford remarked. "His art made you like people of all ages or positions in life as you smiled, laughed, sympathized, or cried. Norman Rockwell's art always indelibly reflected America as it was at its best."

In June 1993, the new, enlarged Norman Rockwell Museum at Stockbridge, with hundreds of original canvases and drawings, was officially opened on a beautiful, spacious site.

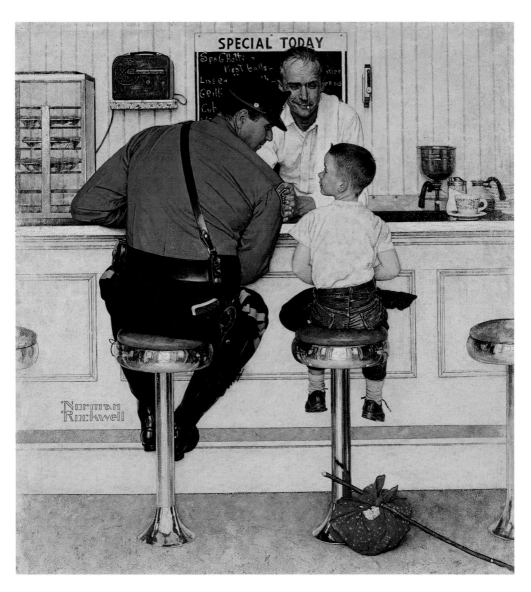

Norman Rockwell drew from boyhood experiences to paint *The Runaway* in 1958.

Norman's actual studio, much as he left it, has been erected on the grounds.

Remembering Norman Rockwell for his "freshness, humor, tenderness," the museum's director, Laurie Norton Moffatt, said "he chose his niche, he loved it and was exceedingly gifted at it. As an illustrator, he was able to remain current for sixty-five years, which really is remarkable."

Movie director Steven Spielberg, a major patron of the museum, said in an interview with *Berkshire Magazine*, "My love of Norman Rockwell is apparent in a lot of my films . . ." among them *E.T.*, especially in the close-ups of E.T. and Elliott, "with his ruddy cheeks and deep welling eyes of optimism." And in Spielberg's *Empire of the Sun*, the boy, Jim, saves a copy of *Freedom from Fear* throughout the years he is a prisoner of war. It is the one reminder of his parents putting him to bed at the film's beginning.

"I think we still yearn for the togetherness of the family, the solidarity of the American workforce" that Norman Rockwell portrayed, Spielberg said. "I miss that kind of America that I have never experienced as an American. I miss that face on America."

That "face" was evident at the museum's opening, when, with many former models in attendance, children paraded, Rockwell's sons planted a tree in his memory, and the crowd sang "America the Beautiful." It was a scene out of a Norman Rockwell painting.

As the *New York Times* later described it:

The sun was shining brightly, of course. The sky was blue and the weather was temperate. There were Boy Scouts and Girl Scouts, Kiwanians and Rotarians, antique fire engines and a four-clown band. It was an All-American day. A Norman Rockwell day.

PUPPY LOVE, COMPLETED IN 1926, IS ONE OF NORMAN ROCKWELL'S BEST-KNOWN AND BEST-LOVED ILLUSTRATIONS.

PLACES TO VISIT

There are many places that you can visit to learn more about Norman Rockwell and his work.

The Norman Rockwell Museum at Stockbridge

Stockbridge, Massachusetts 01262
(413) 298-4100

Has the largest collection of Norman Rockwell originals (over five hundred paintings and sketches) and Norman Rockwell's last studio.

The Norman Rockwell Museum

601 Walnut Street
Philadelphia, Pennsylvania 19106
(215) 922-4345

Has all of Norman Rockwell's *Saturday Evening Post* covers in the Curtis Publishing Building, where Norman Rockwell sold his first *Post* cover.

National Museum of the Boy Scouts of America

Murray State University
P.O. Box 9
Murray, Kentucky 42071
(502) 762-3383

Has many Norman Rockwell originals for *Boys' Life* and Boy Scout calendars.

Mark Twain Home and Museum

208 Hill Street
Hannibal, Missouri 63401
(573) 221-9010

Has Norman Rockwell paintings that illustrated special editions of Mark Twain's *Tom Sawyer* and *Huckleberry Finn.*

National Air and Space Museum

Sixth Street and Independence Avenue, S.W.
Washington, D.C. 20560
(202) 357-2700

Has Norman Rockwell paintings for the U.S. space program.

The Norman Rockwell Exhibit

Route 7A
Arlington, Vermont 05250
(802) 375-6423

Has one thousand collotype prints of Norman Rockwell's work and a short Academy Award–winning film, which Rockwell narrates.

FOR FURTHER READING

Buechner, Thomas. *Norman Rockwell: Artist and Illustrator*. New York: Harry N. Abrams, 1970.

Finch, Christopher. *Fifty Norman Rockwell Favorites*. New York: Random House, 1991.

————. *Norman Rockwell's America*. New York: Harry N. Abrams, 1975.

Murray, Stuart, and James McCabe. *Norman Rockwell's Four Freedoms*. Stockbridge, Mass.: Berkshire House, 1993.

Rockwell, Norman, as told to Tom Rockwell. *My Adventures as an Illustrator*. New York: Doubleday, 1960.

INDEX

Page numbers in *italics* indicate illustrations.

ABOUT THE AUTHOR

Joel H. Cohen has published thirty books, most of them for young readers and most with or about prominent athletes and entertainers such as Hank Aaron, Jim Palmer, Bill Cosby, and Lucille Ball. His articles have appeared in various magazines and newspapers, including *Sports Illustrated for Kids*, *Scholastic Scope*, *American Girl*, *TV Guide*, *Parents*, and the *New York Times*. Mr. Cohen and his wife, Nancy, have four children and live in Staten Island, New York.